RAILWA
WARTIME

Tim Bryan

SHIRE PUBLICATIONS

Published by Shire Publications Ltd,
PO Box 883, Oxford, OX1 9PL, UK
PO Box 3985, New York, NY 10185-3985, USA
Email: shire@shirebooks.co.uk   www.shirebooks.co.uk

First published 2011.
Transferred to digital print on demand 2014.

A CIP catalogue record for this book is available from the
British Library.

Shire Library no. 647   •   ISBN-13: 978 0 74781 050 6

Tim Bryan has asserted his right under the Copyright,
Designs and Patents Act, 1988, to be identified as the
author of this book.

Designed by Tony Truscott Designs, Sussex, UK
Typeset in Perpetua and Gill Sans.
Printed and bound by PrintOnDemand-Worldwide.com,
Peterborough, UK

COVER IMAGE
In the Second World War railways found themselves on the
front line with staff and facilities suffering badly from the
effects of enemy bombing. This painting by Norman
Wilkinson vividly illustrates the dangers of working on
railways in wartime showing the LMS marshalling yard at
Willesden during an air raid in September 1940.

TITLE PAGE IMAGE
This First World War propaganda photograph, taken
'somewhere in England', shows a woman shunter
signalling to the driver of a Lancashire and Yorkshire
Railway locomotive. (IWM Q28204)

CONTENTS PAGE IMAGE
Soldiers rescued from Dunkirk being served with
refreshments at Kensington Addison Road station (now
Kensington Olympia) on 31 May 1940. (IWM H1633)

ACKNOWLEDGEMENTS
I am grateful to the following for their assistance during
the completion of this book: Elaine Arthurs, Collections
Officer at STEAM; Museum of the GWR in Swindon,
Roger Trayhurn, Swindon Library and the staff of the
Imperial War Museum photographic library. I would also
like to thank Ian Coulson and Niall Clutton who helped
find images for the book. As always, I am grateful to my
wide Ann for her encouragement and for reading and
checking the manuscript.

I am grateful to the following for permission to
reproduce illustrations in the book:
Niall Clutton, page 27 (bottom); IT Coulson Collection,
pages 4, 38, 39, 40 (top/bottom), 41 (top/bottom), 42,
58; Getty Images, page 14; Great Western Society, page
43; Imperial War Museum, title page, contents page,
pages 6, 8, 10 (top), 11, 12 (both), 15, 16, 24 (both),
25, 26 (bottom), 28, 30 (top), 31 (bottom two), 35
(bottom), 46, 47, 48, 59, 61 (top); National Library
of Scotland, page 20; private collections, pages 50
(top/bottom) 54; Science & Society Picture Library, cover,
pages 30 (bottom), 44 (bottom); STEAM: Museum of the
GWR, pages 10, 17, 18, 19, 22, 23, 26 (top), 31 (bottom
two), 32, 33, 34 (top right/bottom) 35 (top) 37, 38,
44, 45, 51, 52, (top) 53, 55, 57, 60; Michael Wyatt,
page 31 (top).

All other pictures are from the authors collection.

Shire Publications is supporting the Woodland Trust, the UK's leading woodland conservation charity, by funding the dedication of trees.

CONTENTS

" For all YOU *know we might be Clapham Junction."*

INTRODUCTION

THE STRATEGIC importance of railways in Great Britain had been recognised by government as early as 1842 with the passing of the Railway Regulation Act, an 'Act for better regulation of Railways and for the Conveyance of Troops', requiring railways to transport troops, ammunition and equipment when required to do so by the War Office. These new powers had as much to do with the prevention of civil disorder in Britain as with ensuring the rapid movement of troops embarking on overseas campaigns. Further minor legislation followed, but more dramatic was the passing in 1871 of the Regulation of the Forces Act, which enabled the government to take full control of the railways in an emergency but still left day-to-day operational control to the railway companies.

Although the first example of troops being carried by train on active service had been on the Liverpool & Manchester Railway soon after its opening in 1830, the first significant use of railways in military campaigns took place in mainland Europe and the United States. In the American Civil War President Abraham Lincoln was quick to see that railways were of great strategic importance, and he put them under government control when war broke out. Both sides in that conflict used railways to move troops around the country. In Europe, Austrian, Prussian and Russian forces had been moved by train in 1849 to defend Vienna but it was not until 1870, during the Franco-Prussian War, that the use of railways by the military on a large scale was pioneered.

In Britain troops bound for the Crimean War did travel by rail but the conflict had little effect on the day-to-day running of railways in Britain. The war was the first occasion that a railway was built specifically for military purposes. More than three thousand British navvies constructed a 6-mile line that was used to transport troops and stores from the port at Balaclava to British encampments at Sevastopol.

The Boer War had a greater effect on railways at home and in South Africa. The government chose not to invoke the 1871 Act, and control of railways remained with the railway companies, who worked with the

Opposite:
During the Second World War, station name boards were painted over to confuse possible invaders, a move that proved problematic for travellers, as this wartime cartoon shows.

5

Royal Navy bluejackets from HMS *Terrible* pose in front of an armoured train at Durban during the Boer War. The wagon has a searchlight that has been improvised from a signal lamp. (IWM Q115145)

Admiralty and the War Office to co-ordinate troop movements. The London & South Western Railway (LSWR) bore the brunt of the work, moving most of the half million troops involved in the campaign from Waterloo to Southampton. In South Africa it soon became apparent that railways would play a key part in the fighting, and, whilst British forces used armoured trains to maintain lines of communication, the guerrilla tactics of Boer forces showed how vulnerable railways could be to attack in wartime conditions.

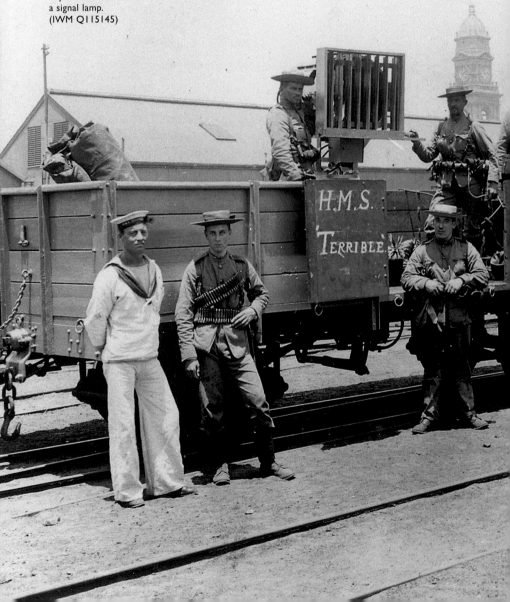

THE HOME FRONT, 1914–18

WHEN BRITAIN declared war on Germany on 4 August 1914 there were already arrangements in place for the government to take control of railways through provisions in the 1871 Regulation of the Forces Act. The Railway Executive Committee (REC), originally created in 1912, was tasked with the 'efficient running of railways' and included the general managers of all the largest railways, nominally under the chairmanship of the President of the Board of Trade. In practice the committee was managed by Herbert Walker, General Manager of the LSWR, and, although in the early months of the war the REC operated almost continuously, day-to-day matters were eventually delegated to individual railways, allowing REC meetings to be held weekly.

One of the first decisions of the committee was to negotiate a financial settlement with the government. The compensation package for railways was based on their 1913 earnings, although there were further concessions for companies such as the LSWR, which, because of their geographical location and size, carried more military traffic than smaller and more remote lines, whose contribution was of necessity less.

With the outbreak of war, prearranged plans came into operation to assist in the mobilisation of reservists and to return Territorial Army units from summer camps to their bases. From 4 August the railways ran extra trains night and day, and within a week the first divisions of the British Expeditionary Force (BEF) were being transported to Southampton Docks. Between 10 and 31 August, 670 special troop trains were run by the LSWR, with the assistance of the Great Western Railway (GWR), along with further trains loaded with ammunition, horses, petrol and stores. This operation continued well into the autumn, and by October the GWR alone had moved more than 360,000 troops from its stations. Initially at least, the dispatch of the BEF was achieved with little disruption to railway timetables, although some goods services were temporarily suspended.

The scale of work carried out by railways in support of the war effort was considerable. Unlike in the 1939–45 conflict, road transport was still in its

Opposite:
A heavily laden American soldier about to board an LSWR train on his way to Southampton in 1918.
(IWM Q31217)

Below: A poster issued by the London & North Western Railway at the outbreak of the First World War in August 1914, giving notice of its takeover by the Railway Executive Committee. (IWM 1244)

LONDON & NORTH WESTERN
RAILWAY.

NOTICE TO STAFF.

The Government has decided to take over the control of the Railways of Great Britain in connection with the Mobilization of the Troops and general movements in connection with Naval & Military requirements. The management of the Railway and the existing terms of employment of the staff will remain unaltered, and all instructions will be issued through the same channels as heretofore.

Euston Station,
August, 1914.

ROBERT TURNBULL,
General Manager.

Private and not for Publication.   NOTICE No. 186

GREAT WESTERN RAILWAY.
(For the use of the Company's Servants only.)

NOTICE OF SPECIAL TRAINS

for the conveyance of

MILITARY TRAFFIC

from

ARMY MANŒUVRES

SEPTEMBER 26th, 27th, 28th and 29th, 1913.

The greatest importance is attached to the punctual working of the Trains shewn in this Notice, and all concerned must carefully read and act upon the instructions contained therein. The hearty co-operation of every Member of the Staff concerned is desired in successfully carrying out these arrangements.

GENERAL STANDARD INSTRUCTIONS.

For General Standard Instructions to be observed in connection with the running of Special Trains, see "Revised General Appendix to the Book of Rules and Regulations," dated May 1st, 1910.

Acknowledge Receipt to Head of Department.

C. ALDINGTON,
September, 1913.   Superintendent of the Line.

WYMAN & SONS LTD., Printers, Fetter Lane, London, E.C., and Reading.—11558a.

Above right:
The cover of a booklet issued by the Great Western Railway giving details of trains run for military manoeuvres in 1913.

Opposite:
Boy Scouts were used on civil defence duties in the First World War. Some Scouts are seen here guarding a railway bridge and the running lines. (IWM U30604)

infancy and so railways necessarily took much of the strain of moving troops and equipment. With much military activity concentrated around Salisbury Plain, it was not surprising that the LSWR played a major role, running 58,859 special troop trains, carrying a total of 20,223,954 men and 1,477,148 horses. When the United States joined the war in 1917, the company ran an additional 1,695 trains carrying American soldiers from Liverpool and Glasgow, where they had disembarked, onward to the Channel ports. On the GWR 37,283 special military trains were run between 1914 and the end of 1919, with the greatest annual total, 9,076, being in 1915. The large numbers of servicemen travelling put a great strain on the refreshment facilities of railways, and at many stations additional arrangements were made for troops. The first of these was at Banbury, through which many military and ambulance trains passed. In September 1914 a 'Station Refreshment Fund', subscribed to by local well-wishers, was begun, with refreshments supplied by Red Cross nurses and local people. Similar arrangements were soon provided at Birmingham, Chester, Exeter and other stations.

Boy Scouts handing out cigarettes and chocolate to American soldiers at Winchester station in 1918. (IWM Q31215)

The Staff Train at Charing Cross in 1918. This painting by Alfred Hayward shows officers waiting to board the daily train that ran from London to the Channel ports. (IWM ART1881)

As well as troop, munitions and fuel trains, the railways also handled thousands of ambulance trains carrying injured servicemen, wounded on the Western Front and elsewhere, from south coast ports to locations all over the network. During the war there were 196 receiving stations to which military ambulance trains carried the sick and wounded from the ports of Dover and Southampton. The list included stations in Scotland and the north of England, although most were concentrated in the south of England, on the lines of the GWR and LSWR. Ambulance trains for domestic use were provided by railways including the Great Central, Great Eastern, Great Western, Lancashire & Yorkshire, London & North Western, London & South Western and Midland companies.

By April 1919 the total number of sick and wounded, including prisoners of war and dominion troops, transported by the railways was 2,680,000. Following the carnage of the Battle of the Somme in the first week of July 1916, the railway handled over 47,000 wounded on ambulance trains, the highest total of the war. Although most wounded soldiers had been taken to Dover or Southampton for repatriation, Avonmouth Docks were also used, especially for troops arriving back from the Mediterranean and the Far East.

As well as supporting the war effort through the movement of troops, railways also played a key role in keeping the British naval fleet supplied with coal. Most of this coal was produced in South Wales and, when the war began, the Admiralty hired around four thousand wagons to shift it from mines to

The interior of a GWR-built 'continental' ambulance train. A set of postcards showing the interior and exterior of the train was issued by the company.

WARD CAR
(Shewing Two Beds arranged for Sitting up Cases)
Continental Ambulance Train—
Built at G.W.R Works, Swindon 1915

The official photographer has captured the hustle and bustle of Victoria Station following the arrival of a LSWR train crammed with soldiers and nurses home on leave from the Western Front. Three signs read 'French money exchanged here for officers and soldiers in uniform'. (IWM Q 30511)

The Great Western provided 238 carriages for ambulance train use in the First World War. This view shows one of the continental trains outside Swindon works.

ports in South Wales. When German submarines made the moving of coal by sea impossible, it was left to the railways to move the coal north to Grangemouth in Scotland, which was designated as the main base for coaling the fleet in 1915. Many collieries supplying coal for the fleet were situated on the lines of companies such as the Taff Vale, the Rhymney and the Vale of Neath, so Pontypool Road on the Great Western was chosen as the main concentration point for Admiralty coal.

The first northbound train left on 27 August 1914, and by 1918 an average of seventy-nine trains was being run every week, carrying 32,000 tons of coal; towards the end of the war even this amount was not enough, and thirty more specials a week were operated, with the highest total being 56,000 tons in one week. Coal trains, nicknamed 'Jellicoe Specials' after Earl Jellicoe, the Admiral of the Fleet, were hauled by the Great Western as far as Warrington, with the London & North Western and Caledonian railways continuing the journey northwards. The scale of the operation was enormous; by the end of the war more than 13,600 loaded coal trains had been run, carrying an estimated 5 million tons of coal. With so much coal being used by the Admiralty and the War Office, railways faced serious shortages during the conflict, especially when the government asked them to cut back consumption to aid the war effort. For railways with extensive route networks, such as the GWR and LNWR, this caused difficulties, especially running large numbers of trains for the military.

REC plans also included an emergency traffic scheme set up in late 1914 to counter a potential invasion threat by German forces on the east coast. The scheme included the production of special timetables and the identification of standard routes that would allow stock from all railways to pass safely in

A train full of wounded soldiers pauses at Birmingham Snow Hill station in 1918. The painting by J. H. Lobley shows nurses providing the troops with food and mugs of tea. (IWM ART3717)

an emergency. The danger of invasion passed, but one part of the scheme that was inaugurated was the daily 'Naval Special' from Euston to Thurso, which ran each weekday linking London and naval bases in the north and east of Scotland. With a route of 717 miles, the train was the longest through train to be regularly run in Britain; in summer the journey time was around twenty-two hours, with naval personnel joining the train at intermediate stations such as Crewe, Preston and Edinburgh.

With the fleet based in the north of Scotland, the Caledonian and Highland railways experienced traffic far in excess of pre-war levels. Apart from the Jellicoe Specials, both railways ran many additional trains for naval personnel, as well as freight services carrying mines and shells, anchors, cables and other equipment. The Caledonian station at Quintinshill in Dumfriesshire was the scene of the worst railway accident of the war on 22 May 1915, when a troop train carrying Territorial soldiers from the Royal Scots crashed into a local train. The gas-lit wooden carriages of the troop train burst into flames; 226 people died in the ensuing inferno, and more than 250 were injured.

Medical orderlies, watched by nurses, load casualties wounded at Passchendaele in 1917 on to an ambulance train. (IWM CO18101)

Several military and railway personnel are present as a tank is loaded on to a wagon for transit to one of the Channel ports.

Railways also ran thousands of special freight trains directly related to the war effort; industrial complexes on the LNWR network produced some of the deadliest loads, including over 10 million tons of TNT from Queensferry near Chester, nearly 11 million hand grenades from West Yorkshire, and several million tons of poison gas from Runcorn. The final destinations for much of this traffic were Channel ports nearest to the Western Front, on the London Brighton & South Coast, London, South Eastern & Chatham and London & South Western railways, including Dover, Folkestone, Newhaven, Plymouth and Southampton.

The huge demands being placed on these ports led to the creation of a new facility at Richborough near Ramsgate. By 1916 millions of tons of stores and thousands of troops were using the port, and in 1918 it became the English terminal of a new cross-Channel train-ferry service that consisted of three steamers, each capable of handling over fifty wagons on its train deck. In the final months of the war it also transported locomotives, tanks and other armoured vehicles. Many of the troops departing for France did so through the port of Southampton, which early in the war was designated 'No. 1 Military Embarkation Port'. The whole dock area was closed to civilians for the duration of the war, and LSWR trains brought troops directly to the quayside for embarkation.

Some of the troopships leaving Southampton and other south coast ports were railway-owned steamers that had been requisitioned by the War Office. When war broke out, there were fourteen railway companies that owned ships; the government and the REC, invoking the 1871 Regulation of Forces Act, took control of 218 vessels, although only 126 were eventually pressed into service. The steamers requisitioned were used in a variety of roles, including as minesweepers, coal transports, convoy ships and ambulance tenders. More than thirty ships were lost, many being torpedoed by German submarines in the English Channel or the Mediterranean.

For the civilian population, travel by rail became progressively more difficult as the conflict wore on. After the mobilisation of the BEF in 1914 the railways attempted to minimise inconvenience to the traveller, but as it became clear that the war would not end swiftly, they were forced to introduce unpopular changes to their timetables. In early 1915 the running of excursion trains and some Sunday services was abandoned and cheap fares were suspended. Despite these measures, ordinary trains remained very crowded, especially at holiday periods, even though in 1916 the government cancelled both the Spring and August bank holidays. Further discouragement was effected by the raising of fares and restrictions on the amount of luggage that could be carried. Passenger mileage did fall from over 31 million in 1914 to under 20 million by 1918 but, as the war situation grew more serious, appeals to the public not to travel increased and the measures adopted became more draconian. Even a 50 per cent increase in fares had only a

One of the train ferries that ran to and from the Continent. An American ambulance train is being loaded. On the right, a number of motor lorries have already been chained ready for the voyage.

limited effect on numbers travelling, and the railways struggled to cope with demand from a population clearly worn down by four years of war but who still wanted to travel, perhaps to forget the horrors of the conflict, if only for a short time.

Although trains were crowded and lacked facilities, railway travellers in the First World War did not have to contend with the effects of German bombing and the blackout to any great extent. During the course of the war there were only 108 air raids on targets in Britain, and the level of air-raid precautions undertaken was primitive in comparison with those adopted in 1939. Not until over three months after the outbreak of war were notices fixed to the windows of carriages asking passengers to close blinds at night, following comments from British pilots who had noticed that lighted trains made ideal guides for enemy bombers to follow from the coast to London. These notices were requests rather than instructions and thus were often ignored by passengers. Unsurprisingly, railway premises in London were hit by German bombing, with Liverpool Street and St Pancras being badly damaged. Many raids also targeted locations in East Anglia and the north-east, and the Great Eastern Railway suffered the most casualties. In all, twenty-four railwaymen were killed whilst on duty in Britain, and another ninety-seven injured.

A number of GWR ships were requisitioned for use during the war, including the SS *St Patrick*, which normally operated the Fishguard–Rosslare route.

HOME AND ABROAD, 1914–18

WITHIN WEEKS of the dispatch of the BEF in 1914, it became apparent that urgent requests for equipment and munitions could not always be answered by the use of existing manufacturing capacity. As a result, the Railway Executive Committee began approaching railway companies with requests for the production of equipment for the military. On 2 September 1914 an urgent call for the production of 12,250 ambulance stretchers was answered by eleven railway companies, which divided the work between them. This informal arrangement continued with a further order for five thousand general service wagons, but in October 1914 the President of the Board of Trade approached the LNWR with a view to seeking railway assistance in production of shells and other munitions.

Although the initial approach was through the LNWR, it was a more general plea for assistance. In 1914 little was known outside Woolwich Arsenal about shell production, but the LNWR's Locomotive Superintendent, Charles Bowen-Cooke, knew Sir Frederick Donaldson, the Director of Ordnance, and, following a meeting, drawings were handed over detailing the equipment required. On 20 October 1914 Bowen-Cooke met with other railways' Chief Mechanical Engineers to clarify what was required. With requests for assistance from the War Office intensifying, more formal arrangements were put in place when a sub-committee of the REC was set up to co-ordinate war work.

As the war continued, railway workshops were called on to manufacture all manner of munitions and equipment. With their well-equipped facilities and skilled and adaptable staff, such works as Crewe, Derby, Doncaster and Swindon were more than capable of rising to any challenge set them by the War Office. Early in the war, Crewe works received an urgent order to construct what became the first armoured train to be built in the First World War. Described as a 'mobile pillbox', and equipped with machine-guns and small arms, the train could move at the speed of an express goods train and consisted of two gun vehicles and two infantry vans, with a locomotive marshalled in the middle. Two of these trains were eventually completed,

Opposite:
First World War soldiers in a railway wagon. No fewer than seven Allied soldiers pose for the photographer on the remains of a railway wagon riddled with bullet holes. The picture was taken on the Somme in 1918.

Half of one of the armoured trains built at Crewe. A further two vehicles would have been coupled to the back of the train, which was propelled by a GNR 0-6-2 tank engine shrouded in armour.

with one stabled on the Norfolk coast and the other north of Edinburgh, but neither saw any real action in the course of the war.

Shortages of ammunition on the Western Front in 1915 led to a dramatic rise in munitions production at workshops. Millions of fuses, shells and shell cases were produced, and also cartridge cases used on the front line were reformed and repaired. By 1916 it was reported that eight works were collectively repairing over 200,000 cases a week, a figure that increased to over 375,000 by June the following year. Works such as Swindon and Crewe also built gun carriages, limbers and mountings for the Army, as well as equipment for the Admiralty such as grapnels, anchors, mines and boat fittings.

Whilst the huge contribution made to the war effort was of national importance, it did mean that pre-war maintenance levels declined and

Many railway works became munitions factories in the First World War. The shells in this picture await loading at Swindon Works in 1915; the wagon shown is a GWR 'Iron Mink' gunpowder van, built entirely of steel with a wooden 'non-spark' lining to prevent explosion or fire.

backlogs built up in the locomotive department, with engines running longer mileages between overhauls. This and the postponement of permanent-way renewals may have been the cause of a serious accident on the LNWR on 14 August 1915. A hurriedly replaced locomotive crank pin fell out, causing a coupling rod to detach south of Weedon in Northamptonshire, pushing the track out of alignment and derailing the following train, the Euston to Holyhead Irish Mail, killing ten passengers and injuring twenty-one.

By the end of the war the railways were in a very run-down state. Matters were made worse by the severe shortage of staff caused by the cumulative effects of conscription during the conflict. The euphoria following the declaration of war in August 1914 meant that British railway companies struggled hard to retain staff as thousands flocked to join the colours. By November recruiting officers were required to request a certificate from railwaymen enlisting to prove that they had permission to do so from their company. This enabled railways to maintain enough staff to run not only all the military traffic they were now having to deal with, but also ordinary goods and passenger services.

In March 1915 General Kitchener asked the REC to report on what the minimum number of staff needed to run the railway network safely might be, as further men were needed for the war effort. A year later the war situation had not improved, and all unmarried men between the ages of eighteen and forty-one became liable for enlistment. Identification cards were issued to those in essential posts, such as signalmen, footplate staff and shunters, to prove that they were not required for call-up. Within months the situation had worsened still further and railways were forced to release all men under twenty-six except those in vital jobs. The offensive of early 1918 required yet more men, and the railways became seriously understaffed. The steadily decreasing workforce had been augmented during the war by the re-employment of retired staff, the payment of overtime to those who remained, and the employment of women in many posts. At the height of the war, more than 55,000 women worked on the railways, mainly as porters, ticket collectors, messengers and carriage cleaners, although many were also employed in railway workshops on munitions work. On the Great Western 6,345 women worked on the railway, of whom 2,900 were employed in clerical positions.

In the early years of the conflict, the huge efforts made by British railway companies in moving men, munitions and equipment to Channel ports were mirrored by similar support from French railways to transport not only their own troops but also those of the British Expeditionary Force. The sheer scale of the demands made on French and Belgian railways was compounded by the relentless advance of German forces and the destruction of locomotives and

Railways issued badges like this one to vital railway staff who could not be conscripted into the forces, in order to protect them from the attention of women who might present them with white feathers in the mistaken belief that they were cowards shirking their duties.

rolling stock. By 1916 the situation had reached crisis point and Eric Geddes, Deputy General Manager of the North Eastern Railway, was appointed by David Lloyd George, the Secretary of State for War, to investigate the transportation of Allied forces on the Western Front.

The report, compiled after a visit to France, did not make comfortable reading for the War Office. It noted that arrangements then in place were shambolic. It recommended that between two and three hundred locomotives and up to twenty thousand wagons would be required within three months, along with almost 1,000 miles of track, and railway staff to maintain them, or else the whole transportation system for the British Army in France could break down completely. At the end of November 1916 the Railway Executive Committee began to undertake the work to ensure that the recommendations of the report were implemented. By moving only the most essential freight and pooling their rolling stock, the goods departments of British railways were able to supply the required twenty thousand wagons for use overseas, although they were not delivered until the end of 1917.

Health and safety measures are absent in this image of a female gas-lamp cleaner at work at Manchester Victoria station on the LNWR. (IWM Q109866)

A female porter checks the number of Great Central Railway 'Director' 4-4-0 which was still very new, having been built in 1913. (IWM Q28014)

To provide the track required, eleven railways converted double-track lines to single-track and closed little-used branch lines, such as the Basingstoke & Alton Light Railway, and the Coleford branch of the GWR. In addition, the REC also called for another army, this time of platelayers, who were recruited from a number of railways and sent to France in December 1916 to carry out urgent repairs and rebuilding away from the front line. The men were organised into eight companies and, although working for the War Office, remained civilians. Many large railways did, however, have their own Royal Engineer companies consisting of enlisted staff who carried out repair and maintenance work nearer the front.

The initial request for around three hundred locomotives for use overseas soon proved inadequate, and the total sent abroad was eventually more than a thousand. More than half this total comprised Great Central Railway 2-8-0 heavy freight engines built for the War Department's Railway Operating Division (ROD). The Robinson-designed O4 class proved both powerful and easy to maintain and was produced not only by the Great Central but also by locomotive builders such as Kitson, North British and Robert Stephenson & Company. The remaining engines supplied for War Department use were loaned to the government by British railways and sent to locations well away from their usual haunts, such as Egypt, Mesopotamia, Palestine and Salonika. The LNWR supplied by far the largest number, providing 111 0-6-0 and 0-8-0 tender

Two Railway Operating Division (ROD) locomotives. The wrecked engine is a Robinson O4 class 2-8-0. There is no indication as to whether the locomotive was derailed as a result of enemy action or by accident. (IWM Q10005)

engines for the war effort. The GWR provided seventy-three locomotives, including some very elderly 0-6-0 'Armstrong Goods' and 'Dean Goods' engines, as well as more modern 43xx 2-6-0 freight locomotives. Other companies, including the LSWR, the North Eastern, the North British, the Great Central and the Midland, also provided stock, with the smallest contribution coming from the London Brighton & South Coast Railway, which supplied eight 0-6-2 'Radial' tank engines. In all 516 locomotives were loaned to the War Department, and by 1921 all but fifty-three had been returned. Some of them never returned home, including six GWR 'Dean Goods' engines withdrawn in Salonika.

Robinson ROD 2-8-0 no. 1631 on 'active service' in France. This example was built by Kitson and Company of Leeds in 1918, and a small plate above the smokebox door of the engine reads '*Depot d'attache blargies*'. On its return the engine was hired to the GWR before eventually being sold to the LNER in 1924.

On the Western Front, as larger numbers of locomotives were provided from England, their introduction led to the ROD running an increasing number of troop trains in northern France on well over 800 miles of track formerly operated by the Nord company. Away from the main lines, which in many cases ran close to the battlefields, the Allies operated an extensive network of narrow-gauge 'field' railways, which linked the standard-gauge railheads with artillery positions and the trenches themselves. Construction of these lines began in 1916, and by the end of the war more than 800 miles

Narrow-gauge railways were used to transport troops and equipment to the front line, but also to evacuate the wounded during and after battles. Troops from the 27th Brigade, 9th Division, are here being moved from Meteren to medical units behind the front line in August 1918. (IWM Q6959)

of track were in use. British forces used a variety of steam locomotives, as well as Simplex petrol tractors, to haul trains, which often carried shells, poison gas, cement, barbed wire, timber, concrete and, on occasions, troops travelling to and from the front line. The proximity of these railways to the front line meant that they were often damaged by enemy shelling and thus in a poor condition.

The widespread jubilation and relief felt by railway staff at the end of the war was tempered by the effects of four years of conflict. Apart from the obvious human cost of the war, the enormous upheaval it caused had left the railways in a very run-down condition. The total number of staff who had enlisted during the war was 184,475 – 49 per cent of the total staff of military age in 1914. Those staff not called up for military service were exhausted, and the railways needed considerable investment to return their operations to pre-war standards. By 1921 it was estimated that more than 21,500 railwaymen had been killed in the conflict, and their contribution was marked by memorials and rolls of honour at stations and depots all over the railway network.

The Victory Arch at Waterloo Station was built between 1919 and 1922 as a memorial to the 585 London & South Western Railway employees who were killed in the First World War. The triumphal arch is monumental in scale, almost three storeys high and a magnificent tribute to the railway men who gave their lives in the war.

EVACUATION
AND INVASION

A FTER THE First World War, Britain's railways endured almost two decades of strife and upheaval. The 1921 Railways Act replaced the 120 smaller railway companies then in existence with the 'Big Four' companies: the Great Western (GWR), London Midland & Scottish (LMS), London & North Eastern (LNER) and Southern (SR) railways. Following this grouping, railways had to contend with industrial strife, the effects of the Wall Street Crash and the economic depression, and increasing competition from road transport.

By 1938 the uncertain international situation before and after the Munich Crisis had caused railway revenues to drop by almost £2 million; the Railway Executive Committee (REC) was re-established and began to co-ordinate emergency plans that could be put into action at short notice. Work on preparing railways for war had begun at least a year earlier with the establishment of the Railway Technical Committee (RTC), which examined strategic issues such as the protection of railway control centres, air-raid precautions, lighting restrictions and the stockpiling of key supplies.

When the Second World War began on 3 September 1939 the Big Four companies and London Transport came under the control of the Railway Executive Committee, as they had done in the First World War, through the issue of an order under the Emergency Powers (Defence) Act of 1939. The role of the REC in the Second World War was different from that played in the earlier conflict. Acting as a link between the railway companies and government, its function was advisory, with the railways themselves remaining largely under the control of their own management. Housed in a disused London Underground station at Down Street, the Chairman of the REC was Sir Ralph Wedgwood, previously General Manager of the LNER.

Although financial compensation for railways had been settled quickly in the First World War, the same was not the case in the 1939–45 conflict. Although temporary arrangements were put in place in 1940, it was not until the following year that railways were finally given a proper settlement. This amounted to £43 million, a figure based on the net revenues for each company in the years 1935 to 1937. Railways were

Opposite:
Guardsmen
evacuated from
Dunkirk in and
around a Southern
Railway train
at Dover on
29 May 1940.
(IWM H1631)

29

A Ministry of Health official poster giving details of those eligible for evacuation in 1939. (IWM PST0057)

EVACUATION

DETAILS OF FACILITIES ARRANGED FOR

(1) OFFICIAL PARTIES
(TO BILLETS PROVIDED BY THE GOVERNMENT)

Evacuation is available for

SCHOOL CHILDREN
MOTHERS with **CHILDREN** of School Age or under
EXPECTANT MOTHERS

(2) ASSISTED PRIVATE EVACUATION
A free travel voucher and billeting allowance are provided for

CHILDREN OF SCHOOL AGE or under
MOTHERS with **CHILDREN** OF SCHOOL AGE OR UNDER
EXPECTANT MOTHERS
AGED and BLIND PEOPLE
INFIRM and INVALIDS

who have made their own arrangements with relatives
or friends for accommodation in a safer area

✦ FOR INFORMATION ASK AT THE NEAREST SCHOOL

A patriotic poster issued by the Big Four companies. A neutral blue livery was chosen for the locomotive.

IN WAR AND PEACE

WE SERVE

GWR · LMS ⬛ LNER · SR

guaranteed fixed annual payments, with the government agreeing to make up any shortfall, but the government would also keep any surplus. The total amount was £13 million less than the 'standard revenue' amount estimated by the companies themselves, a source of resentment to such companies as the GWR, which had been relatively prosperous in the years before war broke out.

The Munich Crisis had prompted railway companies and government departments to formulate detailed plans for the evacuation of schoolchildren and vulnerable adults from London and other conurbations. The crisis had offered the opportunity for a 'dry run', and the GWR ran more than two hundred trains in an exercise that would be repeated for real a year later. The final plan, which would require the running of more than four thousand special trains, was completed in July 1939. Although the possibility had been discussed that knowledge of these arrangements might cause panic in the civilian population, many details were already well-known to railway staff, and timetables were printed in advance of the actual announcement, which came on 31 August 1939.

The Ministry of Health gave railways just twenty-four hours to put their plans into operation, and from 1 September a huge number of children were moved to safety away from the capital. More than 600,000 people were transported on the first day alone, with London Transport buses and trains connecting with services running from termini and suburban stations. The Great Western Railway moved 112,994 evacuees from the capital in the first four days. The Southern ran more than two hundred evacuation specials, while another fifty trains transported over 35,000 people from the Medway area, where the concentration of docks and naval establishments was seen as a high risk. Similar operations took place in other strategic locations such as Portsmouth, Southampton and Rosyth.

Many of the children had already practised evacuation procedures, but this could hardly have prepared them for the trauma of being separated from their parents and transported many miles away from familiar surroundings. By the end of 1939 over 1.4 million people had been moved from London, along with well over 700,000 from provincial cities such as Birmingham, Glasgow, Liverpool and Sheffield. A less well-known evacuation was the transfer of meat, butter and tea from warehouses in London's docks to locations all over the country. The LMS ran thirty-nine special food trains in early September, including seven carrying 1,600 tons of tea to the north of England.

With the onset of the Blitz, railways were called on to carry out further evacuations from London and other cities, including Bristol. By the end of the war a further million evacuees had been transported, with the last major operation taking place in the summer of 1944, when flying bomb attacks led to thousands fleeing London and the south-east, and the railways running

07224

CT. WESTERN RAILWAY.   SPECIAL TICKET

AVAILABLE FOR ONE PERSON ON DAY OF ISSUE ONLY.
TO BE RETAINED UNTIL COMPLETION OF JOURNEY.

FROM STATION OF ISSUE BY

Gt. WESTERN RLY. TRAIN

AND THENCE TO FINAL DESTINATION

THE STRICT CONDITION OF THE ISSUE OF THIS
TICKET IS THAT THE HOLDER SHALL COMPLY
WITH ALL INSTRUCTIONS GIVEN BY OFFICIALS.

Left: An evacuation ticket issued in 1939. Examples of these scarce tickets are now prized by railwayana collectors.

Below left: A posed but evocative publicity picture of evacuees in a carriage window.

Below: If evacuation was a frightening and upsetting experience for children, it was no less so for mothers like these, watching the departure of their children at Waterloo in 1939. (IWM LN4559C)

2,345 extra trains to locations in the Midlands and the West Country. Early in the war, special casualty evacuation trains were also assembled to move patients from hospitals in London during raids. Eventually thirty-four were brought into use – six GWR, fifteen LMS, ten LNER and three Southern Railway trains were stabled close to London.

The Great Western and LMS also evacuated treasures from the British Museum, the National Gallery, Westminster Abbey and other places to slate mines in North Wales, where they were stored well away from enemy bombs. Just as valuable were the thousands of other loads carried to safety; the contents of entire schools were relocated to the countryside, as were the files and records of businesses and government departments, including the Bank of England.

Before the war railways had made plans to move their headquarters from London to safer locations, and even before the onset of hostilities the GWR began moving its Paddington staff to Aldermaston in Berkshire. The LMS relocated its headquarters to Watford, the LNER to Hitchin, and the Southern to Deepdene House near Dorking, where a network of underground tunnels housed the company's emergency control room.

Less than a year after moving more than a million evacuees, events across the English Channel led to what one writer called the 'greatest troop movement in railway history'. The end of the 'Phoney War' was signalled by the German invasion of Belgium and Holland on 10 May 1940, and within a week it seemed that the British Expeditionary Force might be completely destroyed as it retreated towards the Channel port of Dunkirk. The evacuation of Dunkirk, in what became known as Operation *Dynamo*, began on 26 May, ending nine days later on 3 June. In those nine days, a fleet of naval vessels, steamers, tugs and other small craft evacuated over 300,000 troops, delivering them to the Channel ports.

No amount of planning could have prepared the railways for what was to come, but it was the Southern that was busiest, although during the evacuation there were few places in England not affected. From headquarters at Redhill, staff co-ordinated the movement of trains to and from ports using a pool of 186 locomotives and more than two thousand carriages. Through services were run by the GWR via Andover Junction and

A Great Western lorry, loaded with art treasures, awaits unloading in the darkness of a North Wales slate quarry.

Salisbury, by the LNER through Reading and Banbury, and by the LMS through Addison Road, Kensington.

As ship after ship of tired and dispirited soldiers arrived home, trains were arranged to move them to reception areas all over England. The scale of the operation was staggering. On Friday 31 May seventy-six trains carrying over seventy thousand troops were run, and over the whole period well over 200,000 service personnel were moved from the Kent ports of Folkestone, Ramsgate, Dover and Margate, although the LNER was also called on to handle the arrival of over forty thousand men from Dunkirk at Harwich. Weary troops were greeted at many stations along the line by both railway staff and volunteers, who provided them with cigarettes, food and other refreshments.

Even after the end of Operation *Dynamo*, there were more calls on the railways as further evacuations took place at St Valery, Brest, Cherbourg and St Malo. An additional 25,000 civilians were moved from the Channel Islands before they were captured by German forces, along with most of the islands' cattle. By 1940 Britain was isolated but defiant, and the survival and dispersal to bases of over 300,000 troops was due in no small part to the success of what the Ministry of Transport called 'the greatest unpremeditated railway move in history'.

All the main-line railways supplied ships from their extensive fleets for use during the war. This view shows the GWR vessel SS *St Julien* at a South Wales port.

Above: An image taken from *It Can Now be Revealed*: a 1945 booklet about the role of railways in the war. It shows a Home Guard sentry guarding the railway at King's Cross, with an LNER N2 0-6-2 tank engine, complete with condensing apparatus, in the background.

Railway shipping had once again been requisitioned as part of the war effort. Ships from all the Big Four companies were heavily involved in the Dunkirk evacuation, with vessels from the Southern paying a high price for their involvement. Five ships had been sunk by 2 June, and in all twelve were lost. The captain of the GWR ship *St Helier* steered his vessel into Dunkirk harbour under severe shelling on a number of occasions, eventually rescuing over eleven thousand servicemen and refugees. The LMS ship *Scotia* was sunk at Dunkirk and the LMS fleet also took part in the evacuations from St Valery. In the years that followed, the railway fleet was pressed into service as assault

Right: Many railway depots or stations had their own Home Guard battalions. This is one of the GWR's Birmingham battalions on parade.

boats, minesweepers, troop carriers and hospital ships from Iceland to the Mediterranean, taking part in the Anzio and D-Day landings.

Following Dunkirk, events in Europe moved with incredible speed, leaving Britain vulnerable to invasion. Hundreds of railway bridges were mined with explosives so that they could be blown up in the event of an attack. These bridges, stations and other railway property were guarded by Local Defence Volunteers, and soon railway companies had their own dedicated battalions of Home Guard units across the rail network. Pillboxes and other defensive positions were situated along strategic sections of line, station nameboards were painted over or removed, and important items of equipment such as water cranes were marked with red paint to show that they should be immobilised if an invasion took place.

A further measure was to provide twelve armoured trains that could patrol coastal lines on the south coast and in Scotland. Three of these trains, which included First World War vintage rail-mounted guns at either end, along with accommodation for troops, were manned by Polish soldiers when they were brought into use in June 1940. One special train was provided for the narrow-gauge Romney, Hythe & Dymchurch Light Railway in Kent. Situated in a militarised area, the railway, which before the war had carried holidaymakers, was often the target of attack by German aircraft.

Opposite top right: Even in the middle of the Second World War, the bravery of soldiers in the previous conflict was not forgotten, as this image of a woman worker pasting up a poster at Paddington illustrates.

The Prime Minister, Winston Churchill, reading a newspaper as he waits for his train at St Andrews after inspecting Polish troops and naval establishments in Scotland on 23 October 1940. (IWM H4985)

RAILWAYS UNDER ATTACK

L ONG BEFORE the war, the railway companies and the government had anticipated that Britain's railway network would be a major target from air attack. From 1937 a good deal of time and effort, and more than £13 million, were spent on Air Raid Precautions (ARP), with well over £7 million of this total provided by the government. The process began with the training of more than 170,000 staff in ARP duties, and the provision of steel helmets, gas masks and other protective clothing. The terrible effect of poison gas on Allied troops on the Western Front in the First World War was remembered by the authorities, who feared that gas would be used on the civilian population. Specialist training was provided in gas decontamination methods, and specially equipped cleansing vans were deployed at key locations ready to be used at stations or depots where there were no decontamination facilities.

Railways also stockpiled equipment and materials for use in repairing bomb-damaged lines and stations. On the LMS, enough sleepers, rail and spare pointwork to replace 22 miles of track were assembled and stored at various centres on its network. Welding and metal-cutting equipment was also acquired for emergency use, along with mobile cranes and jacking gear. The vulnerability of bridges led to railways keeping large stocks of timber, and in some cases, prefabricated girders, that could be deployed when bomb damage made a bridge unsafe.

Because of the strategic nature of the railway network, trains had to be kept running even when bombs were falling, and so effective communication and control were essential. More than £317,000 was invested in providing duplicates of railway control rooms in reinforced bomb-proof locations that could operate during air raids. Money was also spent on the protection of signal boxes, which were naturally very vulnerable, as they contained so much glass. Some had windows bricked up or covered with steel plates. Another measure adopted involved the covering of glass with hessian or cellophane. In larger stations, to reduce the risk of passengers being badly injured by falling or flying glass, much of the glazing was removed from

Opposite:
An enormous bomb being lifted by an RAF bomb disposal team from a crater at Shepherd's Bush goods depot in west London on 20 February 1944.

Signal boxes were dangerous places in an air raid, as they contained so much glass. In a posed publicity picture, this signalman continues to man his post, wearing a standard-issue gas mask.

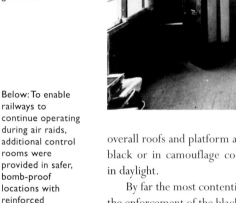

Below: To enable railways to continue operating during air raids, additional control rooms were provided in safer, bomb-proof locations with reinforced concrete roofs, or in cellars of existing buildings.

overall roofs and platform awnings. Where glass did remain, it was painted black or in camouflage colours, making station platforms gloomy even in daylight.

By far the most contentious issue surrounding Air Raid Precautions was the enforcement of the blackout. In 1937 a lighting committee consisting of representatives of the Ministry of Transport, the Air Ministry, the Home Office and the railways agreed emergency lighting restrictions, which came

into force on 1 September 1939. Whilst it was generally agreed that railways could not operate with safety and speed in a complete blackout, one general manager described the restrictions as 'the greatest and most widespread disability they had ever had to meet'. To enable railway operations to continue, all fixed lighting in stations, depots and yards consisted of very low intensity 'fully restricted' lighting that remained on during air raids. The greenish-blue lamps were caustically nicknamed 'gloomy glim' by staff and

Above left:
One of the most difficult and dangerous railway jobs in the blackout was that of the shunter. With so little light, the task of marshalling train loads of freight wagons was not an easy task.

Above right:
A goods guard completing paperwork in the blackout by the light of his hand lamp.

Left: Willesden Goods Yard in 1944. The minimal lighting permissible in the blackout is evident, and one can see why life was so dangerous for the shunters.

Platform 10 at Euston Station in September 1944, showing the working conditions endured by staff in the blackout.

As well as warning passengers about keeping blinds down in the blackout, railways also warned them about the danger of tripping or falling over whilst getting on and off trains at stations.

gave only minimal light; all other lighting was turned off when the sirens sounded, making railway premises dangerous places to be in an air raid. Accident reports kept by the railways for the period show that, as well as serious injuries and deaths caused by German bombing, there were thousands of further accidents that were the result of passengers tripping over discarded luggage or platform trolleys, or by falling from station platforms or trains in the darkness.

There was much debate about blackout arrangements on trains themselves; when war broke out, the new regulations stated that all lamps in the compartments, corridors and lavatories of carriages were to be fitted with a blue bulb that gave out the equivalent of a modern 15 watt bulb, shrouded in a narrow metal cylinder. This led to many complaints from passengers who claimed that these bulbs did not give out enough light even to read by. The government relaxed the restriction in November 1939, replacing the blue bulbs with shaded white lamps in compartments that had carriage blinds closed to keep the blackout at night. Corridors and lavatories continued to be lit by the hated blue lamps throughout the war.

Railway companies also faced the unenviable task of trying to black out locomotive footplates.

Wartime lighting as finally developed in a first-class compartment of an LMS corridor composite carriage.

This was done with canvas anti-glare sheets and steel plates enclosing the cab, and these made the footplate stiflingly hot. Although this measure was usually effective, the glow of the firebox still made locomotives targets for the Luftwaffe. This was only one of the problems facing locomotive crews during air raids, since the blackout also meant that they could not see key landmarks up and down the line. Not surprisingly, it was also hard to spot signals, and difficult to stop a train in just the right place in a blacked-out station. The drivers of electric trains on the Southern faced a different

Anti-glare sheets were provided for locomotive cabs to reduce the glow from fireboxes. This picture shows the arrangement on a LMS 'Jubilee' class engine 'Tanganyika'.

41

challenge in trying to prevent arcing, and so they coasted over points and crossings to keep flash to a minimum. Given the complicated tangle of trackwork around the company's London termini, this was a difficult task. Apart from the relaxation of carriage compartment lighting standards, other restrictions remained in place until 1944.

The extensive planning and preparation carried out before the war were soon needed when the Blitz began. The railways were to attract a great deal of attention from the Luftwaffe and between 1939 and 1944 suffered more than ten thousand air raids, with over 250 incidents reported where lines were put out of action for more than a week. Over fourteen thousand carriages and 24,000 goods wagons were destroyed or damaged. There were many tales of individual heroism by staff who worked bravely to maintain a service during the Blitz; many staff had joined ARP or Home Guard units or became firewatchers to help in the war effort, often carrying out these dangerous and difficult duties after having completed a full shift on the railway. Inevitably, however, the ferocity and frequency of air raids, particularly in the early part of the war, led to casualties amongst railwaymen. The concentrated attacks on the capital in 1940 and 1941 led to damage to all the major London termini, and on the night of 15 October 1940 more than a thousand bombs fell, temporarily closing five main-line stations. On the LNER, Liverpool Street and King's Cross stations were both badly damaged, although Marylebone survived the war with no direct hits.

Sunderland station after a direct hit in the Blitz. Two workmen can be glimpsed right at the very top of the roof inspecting the girders for damage.

With its extensive suburban network, the Southern Railway suffered most from enemy bombing. All the company's major stations were badly damaged on numerous occasions; on one night in April 1941 bombing put Charing Cross, Holborn Viaduct, London Bridge, Waterloo and Victoria out of action, a situation repeated a month later, although on that occasion it was Cannon Street and not Holborn Viaduct that was hit. The most bombed section of line in London was the stretch between Waterloo and Queen's Road (now Queenstown Road) station, which was hit ninety-two times between September 1940 and May 1941.

As bombing raids spread all over the country, stations, depots and lines were severely damaged on many occasions. In the West Midlands, both New Street and Snow Hill stations in Birmingham suffered badly, and when Coventry was attacked on 14 November 1940, 122 incidents were reported on LMS property, with forty-two bombs falling on one 3½-mile stretch of track. Despite having to contend with a 60-foot-wide crater, railway staff restored main-line running within four days. Elsewhere, the Great Western Railway's docks in South Wales and stations and goods depots in Bristol, Newton Abbot and Plymouth were also particularly hard hit. York station was badly damaged during one of the 'Baedeker' raids of 1942, when bombs hit both buildings and rolling stock.

Bombing raids were not confined to London and the major cities. A raid on the Devon town of Newton Abbot on 20 August 1940 killed fourteen people, including four GWR staff.

43

Right: A variation on the 'Is your journey really necessary?' theme, asking passengers to travel at off-peak times.

Below: The Railway Executive Committee issued posters to emphasise to travellers that the primary role of the railways was to support the war effort, despite the fact that thousands still wanted to travel, even in difficult wartime conditions.

If your journey is REALLY necessary and you can choose your times travel between 10 & 4

'The principle adopted for transport in wartime is that the needs of war must come first', a British Railways pamphlet issued in 1943 warned. Within weeks of the outbreak of war, railways issued new emergency timetables. Not surprisingly, holiday and excursion trains were suspended, cheap tickets abolished, and the fastest expresses such as the 'Cornish Riviera Limited' and the 'Flying Scotsman' were curtailed or reduced. The now familiar question, 'Is your journey really necessary?' was first expressed as

All Clear for the Guns
ON
BRITISH RAILWAYS

early as 1939 but became more prominent two years later when posters bearing this message appeared all over Britain's railway network. With traditional resorts closed, holiday traffic declined. The difficulties experienced by railway travellers, such as crowded and blacked-out carriages, low train speeds and the removal of station nameboards and lighting, meant that most people took only essential journeys.

As the war progressed, the traveller faced more privations, with the loss of the most basic comforts enjoyed before 1939. In 1942 the General Manager of the GWR reported that more than eight thousand towels had been stolen from trains, and shortages of other necessities such as toilet paper and soap made long-distance travel difficult on all lines. Shortages of food and the need to discourage unnecessary travel meant that restaurant cars were initially reduced in number, and then completely withdrawn in May 1942. For the hungry traveller there was often little nourishing fare to be had at refreshment rooms, which struggled to provide crockery and utensils for their customers.

The Ministry of Transport put pressure on the railways to reduce timetabled passenger trains in order to cope with the huge numbers of military personnel travelling to and from bases all over the network, and the increasing numbers of war workers commuting to and from the munitions

Below left: Although travellers could not be sure that they would be able to find decent food on long trips during the war, some catering facilities did remain, such as this refreshment trolley at Paddington.

Below: A nurse provides assistance to travellers at Paddington. She is being careful to hang on to the empty teacups, since they were in short supply during the war.

A scene repeated
thousands of times
during the Second
World War. A
sergeant, returning
to duty from leave,
waits at a station
'between London
and Scotland'
in 1944.
(IWM 18782)

establishments that sprang up throughout Britain. Service personnel travelling to and from military bases made trains very crowded, especially at holiday periods. One suggestion put forward in 1941 to reduce congestion on trains was the abolition of first class, a move resisted by the railways, although public opinion forced a compromise that first class would be abolished on suburban trains in October 1941. A similar debate ensued about the use of sleeper services, especially on the long-distance routes operated by the LMS, LNER and, to a lesser extent, the GWR. By 1942 the use of sleeping cars was restricted to those travelling on government or military business only.

Railway stations
in wartime were
often the scenes
of tearful
goodbyes. Several
couples embrace
at Euston in 1944.
(IWM D18906)

ONWARD TO VICTORY

DESPITE all the difficulties and hardships caused by air raids and the blackout, Britain's railways played a crucial part in the eventual victory of the Allies in 1945. Contemporary writers called them the 'Fourth Service', although many of their wartime achievements were shrouded in secrecy in the dark days of the war.

Nowhere was this secrecy greater than in railway workshops. At one stage during the war, more than twenty thousand staff from Britain's railways were employed in the production of munitions and other equipment for the war effort. The well-equipped workshops and flexible workforce made them invaluable in answering the call of the War Office for all manner of jobs, often at short notice. As early as 1937, the LMS had been asked by the War Office to assist in the design of a new tank, eventually known as the 'Covenanter', the first of which was built in 1939. Crewe and Horwich works had built well over five hundred tanks by 1942, with the GWR, LNER and Southern contributing many thousands of other component parts, such as gearboxes and turret rings for armoured vehicles.

A far larger proportion of the work done in railway workshops was related to aircraft production. The skilled workers employed in carriage and wagon departments proved well able to manufacture aircraft wings, the LMS making over four thousand pairs of wings for Hurricane and Typhoon fighters and Horsa gliders. The machine shops at Doncaster and Swindon turned out thousands of component parts for aircraft, with the GWR factory at Swindon producing 171,000 parts for Hurricanes at extremely short notice during the Battle of Britain.

The list of tasks carried out and unusual jobs completed was endless. The LNER produced over half a million parts for anti-aircraft guns and a further 200,000 components for fighter aircraft cannon, whilst the GWR and LMS built gun carriages and brake gear for field guns. Barrage-balloon equipment, cranes, life rafts, lorry bodies, bridge parts and even complete bridges were just some of the other war work undertaken. Many tasks were completed in conditions of great secrecy, with few in the busy workshops

Opposite:
Ammunition being unloaded on to the dockside at Hull in 1943 before being moved by the LNER, depicted in a painting by Bernard Hailstone. Railway-owned docks played a crucial role in the war effort. (IWM LD3107)

'Matilda' tanks under construction at the Crewe works of the LMS early in the war. As more American tanks became available, railway workshops concentrated on other war work.

Handley Page Hampden bombers being constructed at the LMS workshops at Derby.

aware of what was being done. One such project was the manufacture of fifty midget submarine superstructures by the Great Western at Swindon in 1942. As they had done in the First World War, railway workshops also supplied ambulance trains for both home and overseas use, having to build

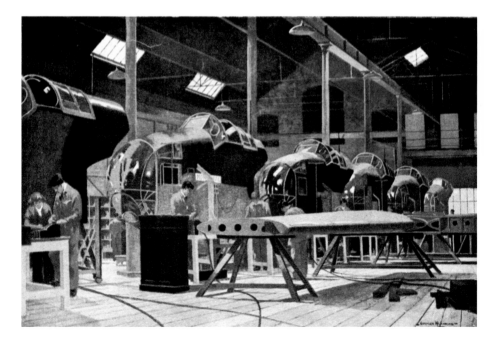

or convert more carriages after the fall of France since a number of trains sent there with the BEF were captured or destroyed during the German advance of 1940.

Railway works also became munitions factories. The LNER turned over one of its works entirely to armaments production, and during the course of the war forged or machined more than 1.5 million shell casings, manufactured over 1.3 million anti-aircraft cartridge cases, and heat-treated 34 million 20-mm cannon shell cases. Many other workshops assisted in a similar way; at Swindon GWR staff produced over sixty thousand bomb casings, including 2,000-pound and 4,000-pound bombs nicknamed 'Goebbels' and 'Goering' by staff to maintain secrecy. As preparations for the invasion of Europe began to take shape, railway works were pressed into service to build landing craft and other boats, with the Southern building more than three thousand, and the GWR at Swindon building a further 150. At the Wolverton carriage works of the LMS 8,442 collapsible assault landing craft were built.

Just after war broke out, R. A. Riddles of the LMS was appointed as the Director of Transportation Equipment at the Ministry of Supply and was made responsible for providing locomotives and rolling stock for use in support of Allied armies in Europe. His first task was to provide an additional ten thousand wagons for use by French railways, and also to provide heavy goods

Many women were employed in railway works manufacturing munitions. Although the woman operating this lathe has a protective hairnet, she does not seem to have any overalls to protect her from the grease and dirt of the workshop.

Landing craft being constructed at Swindon works. The glass rooflights of the factory had been painted out to maintain a blackout, so workers operated under artificial light day and night.

locomotives for use overseas. Given his LMS background, the choice of the Stanier 8F 2-8-0 as a standard type was not a surprise, and orders for three hundred engines were placed with British locomotive builders. When Allied troops were forced to withdraw from France in 1940, the engines were not required and so were loaned to the LMS, before being sent to the Middle East in 1941 and 1942. Two veteran designs used by the War Department in the First World War were once again pressed into service. One hundred GWR 'Dean Goods' engines, by then well over fifty years old, were used, as were ninety-two Robinson 'ROD' 2-8-0s, sent to Egypt and Palestine in 1941.

A 'Dean Goods' locomotive, stabled at Dover following its repatriation from the Continent. It clearly shows signs of hard use in difficult conditions.

Although based on Stanier's 8F 2-8-0 freight design, the later Riddles 'Austerity' design was a rather less elegant solution to the need for powerful, easy-to-maintain locomotives for overseas use.

More modern locomotives designed for War Department use were produced between 1943 and 1945. The 'Austerity' class 2-8-0 and 2-10-0 designs, whilst not the most elegant engines ever built, were powerful and easy to maintain in wartime conditions. Built by the North British Locomotive Company and Vulcan Foundry, both designs were run in in Britain before being sent to Europe after the Allied invasion in 1944. A more radical sight was the appearance of American 2-8-0 and 0-6-0 designs imported into Britain through the ports of Cardiff, Glasgow, Hull and London. Considerable numbers of these engines, built to the British loading

The utilitarian lines of 'USA' 2-8-0 locomotive No. 1604, seen outside the railway workshops at Swindon.

In the Second World War brass and enamel railway service badges were issued to all staff in reserved occupations.

Women cleaning a very dirty LMS 'Coronation' Class Pacific locomotive at its shed at Camden in London.

gauge, were used on freight services by British railways before being taken abroad for use in France, Italy and North Africa. A large number were stabled and prepared at the Great Western's Ebbw Junction workshops, although their basic designs were not to the liking of GWR enginemen more used to Swindon products.

Although staff were once again classified as being in a 'reserved occupation', the workforce of all the Big Four companies was steadily diminished as the conflict wore on, just as it had been in the First World War. After the fall of France in 1940, it was estimated that more than two million men and women would be needed in the armed forces and the munitions industry within twelve months. More and more staff were conscripted, and by the end of the war more than 110,000 were serving with the armed forces or in civil defence. Although staffing levels were increased to attempt to make up this shortfall, the major problem for railways was the loss of skilled labour; many of the men conscripted were very experienced and could not be replaced overnight.

It was only following the employment of thousands of women in railway service that any impression on the staff shortages was made. Before the war around 26,000 women had been employed on Britain's railways, largely as clerks or in catering or cleaning jobs. This figure had grown to well over

124,000 by the end of the war, and female staff found themselves working as porters, ticket collectors, permanent way staff, crane operators and carriage and engine cleaners, although the rapid integration of so many new female staff was not without incident. Old-fashioned attitudes meant that some parts of the railway were slow to take on women, especially locomotive departments, with the result that engine footplates still remained a male preserve. Large numbers of women were, however, employed in railway workshops, carrying out some of the dirtiest and most difficult jobs, such as the operation of steam hammers, machining and welding.

In the difficult years before D-Day, traffic on Britain's railways grew dramatically. In sharp contrast to the First World War, when the majority of Allied troops were on active service overseas, in the Second World War a large proportion of service personnel remained in Britain preparing for the offensives that would eventually come in the later part of the conflict. This put a huge strain on railways, which had the constant task of moving troops and their equipment to take part in large-scale exercises all over the country. Armoured vehicles, ammunition and stores also had to be moved, and by May 1945 railways had run a total of 451,765 special trains for the armed forces.

A further strain was placed on railways by the extra journeys being made by war workers travelling to and from the many new government ordnance factories that were built all around the country to service the war effort. In the build-up to the D-Day invasions in 1944 an extra seven thousand trains a week were run to cope with this demand. Railways also served these establishments by delivering raw materials and collecting the deadly products manufactured there. This work was just part of the huge increase in freight traffic experienced after 1940, affected in no small part by both enemy bombing and submarine activity in the North Sea and elsewhere. By 1944 almost a million wagons were being handled by British railways every week. Much of the coal usually transported by ship around the coast before the war had to be moved by rail instead, and little coal was exported during the war so that production could support home industries and markets. Domestic iron ore production was also dramatically increased, leading to heavy demands being placed on the LMS and GWR in Northamptonshire, Oxfordshire and Rutland.

The huge numbers of travellers generated large quantities of left luggage, as this 1944 picture shows. In addition to the normal paraphernalia left by passengers, military equipment, including helmets, was left behind in the chaos.

Additional responsibilities were placed on railways as the war progressed. In 1942 plans were made to build large numbers of new airfields in the east of England to support a new bomber offensive on Germany. The huge quantities of building materials required for this operation were all carried by rail, with the LNER bearing the brunt of this work. The foundations of many runways were constructed with rubble salvaged from the bomb sites of London, and by the spring of 1943 almost 750,000 tons was delivered by more than 1,700 special trains. Similar special arrangements were needed in July 1943 to ensure that the 14 million bricks required by the Air Ministry were moved from Bedfordshire to East Anglia promptly. Overall, the operation to build and support these new bomber aerodromes involved the movement of over 20 million tons of freight, and also included the conveyance of cement, water pipes and tanks, hangar steelwork, bulldozers and petrol tanks.

Those planning new airfields knew that these bomber bases would also require huge amounts of fuel. For each 'thousand bomber strike' undertaken by the United States Air Force, over 2½ million gallons of petrol would be used, requiring the running of twenty-eight special petrol trains. Much of the fuel was delivered by convoy to west coast ports, and so it fell to the GWR and LMS to run large numbers of petrol trains. In September 1943 the LMS ran 908 specials of this type; with such a dangerous load, these trains were not much liked by footplate staff, especially at the height of the Blitz. As demand increased still further, seven pipelines were eventually built to supply airbases, relieving the pressure on the railways. Even so, demand remained high and in the three months after D-Day in 1944 well over a thousand petrol trains were run to airfields in East Anglia alone.

Many thousands of bombs had already been transported by rail by the time that the bomber offensive began to increase in intensity. More than 300,000 tons of bombs were shifted by the LMS alone in the two years leading up to D-Day, as munitions were moved from the ports to storage depots and finally to airfields. Trains ran day and night as the bombing campaign continued, entailing careful planning to ensure 'bomb specials' arrived promptly.

The perilous nature of transporting such loads was illustrated by an incident that occurred on the night of 2 June 1944. Approaching the town of Soham in Cambridgeshire, driver Benjamin Gilbert looked back from the cab of his WD 2-8-0 to see that the first wagon of his trainload of explosives was on fire. Quickly stopping the train, Gilbert and his fireman uncoupled the engine and wagon and ran forward to the nearby signal box, where they hoped a 'line clear' would allow them to take the wagon well away from the town. Unfortunately the wagon exploded before they could do this, killing the fireman and signalman and badly injuring Gilbert. The heroism of the railwaymen undoubtedly saved the lives of many people in Soham, who would have been killed if the whole train had exploded.

Before D-Day, work done by railways in upgrading the network in the 1930s proved vitally important, along with further wartime upgrades undertaken on behalf of the Ministry of War Transport. These included the doubling and quadrupling of tracks of existing main lines, and the construction of new avoiding lines and connections such as the one between the GWR and the Southern at Plymouth. Railways also built miles of new sidings and loop lines for war factories, as well as stations and halts to serve them. Major work was carried out on railways close to Salisbury Plain and the embarkation points for the invasion. Two cross-country lines on the GWR, the old Midland & South Western Junction and the Didcot, Newbury & Southampton railways, were turned into major routes by lengthening loops and doubling lines where possible.

In the months before the invasion of Europe, the railway network was full of trains heading for the south of England; the transport planning for Operation *Overlord* had begun many months earlier in great secrecy when senior officials from the four main-line companies met to plan in great detail the arrangements for what was to be the railways' 'finest hour'. Locomotive and staff availability, timetabling and restriction of normal services were all discussed to ensure that there would be no last-minute hitches. The railways had already gained considerable experience of transporting large quantities

Most of the major convoys bringing American troops and their equipment to Britain in the period before D-Day arrived at west coast locations, including Liverpool, Cardiff and Newport. American soldiers are seen here disembarking at Cardiff in 1944.

of troops, stores and supplies during the North African campaign and had also grown accustomed to coping with the large numbers of American troops who began to pour into the country in the months before D-Day.

General Montgomery met four hundred representatives of railway staff of all grades in early February 1944, praising their effort, and he urged them on to 'complete victory', a clear sign that the invasion was imminent. Although the date of the invasion was to be 4 June 1944, for railways the operations began in earnest on 26 March, when the large-scale concentration of troops and equipment started. Quiet rural stations in southern England became bustling centres of activity, with many being extended dramatically to cope with the huge influx of military traffic. One unnamed station on the Southern was dramatically transformed in the six months before D-Day with the addition of 14 miles of sidings, with the space to handle over 2,500 wagons.

The American general Dwight Eisenhower addresses South Wales dock workers, thanking them for their enormous contribution to the war effort.

In the two months before D-Day, the railways ran 24,459 special trains for the movement of troops, ammunition and equipment. Regular timetabled passenger services were restricted to allow priority for military traffic, and from the beginning of April the public were forbidden from visiting the south coast because of the invasion build-up, necessitating the suspension of many Southern Railway services. On 10 May alone, eight hundred specials were run to move the stores, armoured vehicles, landing barges and heavy

equipment necessary to support the invasion, a task requiring over thirty thousand wagons. Special arrangements were required to ensure the delivery of more than seven thousand tanks to concentration points near the coast, since many were large 'out of gauge' loads. Amazingly, despite the fact that long trainloads of tanks, guns and other military equipment had been trundling across the railway network in the months before the invasion, few people outside the armed forces, government or railways had much inkling of what was to come. Many of these loads were hidden under sheets and disguised in what some railway staff called the 'Tarpaulin Armada'.

In the weeks before the invasion, staff worked night and day to ensure that the flow of trains continued without delay. The Southern Railway was by far the busiest since its network covered most of the south coast and included the Channel ports, from where much of the invasion fleet left for France. All the railways worked closely together, as many of the trains run involved the movement of men and equipment across long distances. The LMS ran 13,279 trains in the eleven weeks between 26 March and 24 June 1944, transporting large numbers of troops from as far afield as the Highlands of Scotland, and in the same period the LNER ran over seven hundred trainloads of stores and equipment to the London docks.

After the establishment of the Normandy beachheads, work for the railways intensified as Allied forces advanced into France. After the war, it was

Opposite bottom: Tanks being loaded on to railway wagons for transport to Channel ports ready for the D-Day landings. The location is not known, but it was probably somewhere on Salisbury Plain.

Tanks on 'Warflat' railway wagons camouflaged to look like ordinary freight vehicles in 1942. Similar measures were adopted in the run-up to D-Day two years later. (IWM 25192)

argued that the four weeks following D-Day were the busiest ever recorded for British railways. More than seventeen thousand further troop trains were run, along with further moves of equipment, stores and petrol. A rather less welcome task was the handling of a steady stream of ambulance trains, and the running of 167 prisoner-of-war trains between June and August 1944.

Having played a key role in the success of the D-Day landings, railways had yet another obstacle to overcome as they came under attack again in June 1944 when German V1 bombs began to fall on London and other British cities. The first recorded flying bomb hit a bridge on the LNER near Stratford on 13 June, although the real onslaught did not start until a few days later. By the end of August all main-line companies had been affected, the Southern again suffering most damage, with 528 incidents on or near its property. The 'Doodlebug' campaign also took its toll on railway staff; fifty-four were killed and 1,282 injured, but employees worked tirelessly to restore damaged track and stations.

A further consequence of the flying bomb attacks was that railway companies had to embark on another programme of evacuation, which began on 6 July 1944. More than forty thousand people were moved to safer locations in the West Country, the Midlands and the North by the Great Western, although the company and the other railways also had to cope with hundreds of thousands of other 'unofficial' evacuees desperate to escape from

The chaotic scene at Battersea station on 18 June 1944, the aftermath of a V1 'flying bomb' attack.

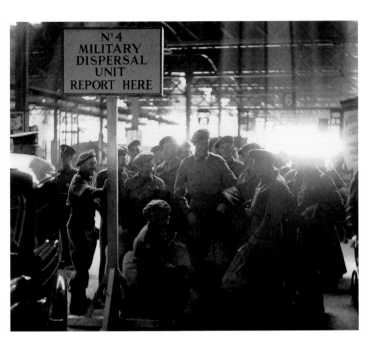

Charing Cross station in 1945, as British soldiers arriving home gather to await further information on their demobilisation. (IWM BU8054)

London. By the end of September it was estimated that railways had transported well over a million people from the capital.

As the Allied victory drew closer, V1 flying bomb attacks dwindled, although the brief and frightening introduction of the deadly V2 rockets in September 1944 again raised tension, especially in London. By December, however, matters had improved enough to allow railway Home Guard units to be stood down. In April 1945 the end of the blackout was greeted with huge relief by staff who had struggled through the war years in difficult conditions; a month later, they were able to celebrate the Allied victory in Europe. Following the end of the war in the East, all the railways ran extra trains to cope with the waves of demobbed troops arriving home, and railway staff looked to the future.

The undoubted success of the railways as Britain's 'Fourth Service' in the war meant that staff and management of all the main-line railways were intensely proud of their achievements and optimistic about the future. In the years following the war, however, they were to face further difficulties, including chronic shortages of coal, staff and other resources, political interference, and freezing weather, ultimately culminating in nationalisation and another new chapter in Britain's railway history.

The cover of *It Can Now Be Revealed*, a publicity brochure issued by the British railway companies in 1945 not only to celebrate their contribution to the war effort, but also to press their case for post-war investment.

"IT CAN NOW BE REVEALED"

MORE ABOUT BRITISH RAILWAYS IN PEACE AND WAR

FULLY ILLUSTRATED

ONE   SHILLING   NET
1945

PLACES TO VISIT

MUSEUMS

Imperial War Museum, Lambeth Road, London SE1 6HZ.
Telephone: 0207 416 5000. Website: www.iwm.org.uk
National Railway Museum, Leeman Road, York YO26 6XJ.
Telephone: 0870 421 4001. Website: www.nrm.org.uk
Steam: Museum of the Great Western Railway, Kemble Drive, Swindon,
Wiltshire SN2 2TA. Telephone: 01793 466646.
Website: www.steam-museum.org.uk

GWR 2-6-0
no. 5322, one of
twenty brand-new
engines sent to
France in 1917
by the company.
Returned to steam
in 2008, the engine
is now based at
Didcot Railway
Centre and is
painted in the
khaki livery of the
Railway Operating
Division.

HERITAGE RAILWAYS

A number of Britain's heritage railways have locomotives and rolling stock
used in both world wars. Some, such as the North Norfolk Railway and the
Severn Valley Railway, run special large and well-attended wartime-themed
events every year. Details of these can be obtained from railway magazines
and publications, or from the Heritage Railways Association website:
http://ukhrail.uel.ac.uk
Of particular interest are:
Didcot Railway Centre, Didcot, Oxfordshire OX11 7NJ.
Telephone: 01235 817200. Website: www.didcotrailwaycentre.org.uk
Didcot is home to both 43xx 2-6-0 no. 5322, built in 1917, and 1940-
built 2-8-0 heavy freight engine no. 3822, shown in wartime livery.

Great Central Railway, Loughborough, Leicestershire LE11 1RW.
  Telephone: 01509 230726. Website: www.gcrailway.co.uk
  Home to GCR Robinson ROD 2-8-0, on loan from the National
  Railway Museum at York.
Keighley & Worth Valley Railway, Keighley, West Yorkshire BD21 5DP.
  Telephone: 01535 645214. Website: www.kwvr.co.uk
  The KWVR is home to four ex-War Department locmotives,
  including a USA 0-6-0 tank engine and an 8F 2-8-0 built by Vulcan
  Foundry in 1945.
Leighton Buzzard Light Railway, Leighton Buzzard, Bedfordshire LU7 4TN.
  Telephone: 01525 373888. Website: www.buzzrail.co.uk
  This narrow-gauge line includes examples of both steam and diesel
  engines used in France by the War Department in the First World War.
Le Petit Train de la Haute Somme, Froissy, 80001 Albert, France.
  Telephone: +33 322 83 11 89. Website: http://appeva.perso.neuf.fr
  A narrow-gauge heritage railway on the last remaining section of
  military lines built by the Allies in the First World War, situated close to
  the Somme battlefield.
Romney, Hythe & Dymchurch Light Railway, Hythe, Kent CT21 6LD.
  Telephone: 01797 362353. Website: www.rhdr.org.uk
  This narrow-gauge railway, which was on the home front line in the
  Second World War, still operates many trains using engines built before
  1939.

FURTHER READING

Bryan, Tim. *The Great Western at War: 1939–1945*. PSL Books, 1995.
Carter, E. F. *Railways in Wartime*. Frederick Muller, 1964.
Gittins, Sandra. *The Great Western in the First World War*. History Press, 2010.
Pratt, Edwin. *British Railways and the Great War*. Selwyn & Blunt, 1921.
Robertson, Kevin. *Britain's Railways in Wartime*. Ian Allan, 2008.
Wragg, David. *Wartime on the Railways*. Sutton Publishing, 2006.

INDEX

Page numbers in italics refer to illustrations